Bitesize Go

# THE EMPER
# NEW CLOTHES
## Tell the truth

*by Alison Hedger*

**Adapted from the traditional tale from Hans Christian Anderson**
**A mixture of narration, mime, rap and song**
**For School Assemblies and End of Term Entertainments**
**KS1 and Lower KS2**
**Approximately 15 minutes**
**The songs are sung by everyone**

This book includes the words and music, a CD containing the story, demonstration versions and backing tracks for all the songs, a recipe and two tricks.
Lyrics and script can be downloaded free of charge from our website at
www.goldenapplemusic.com/bitesize

## THE MUSIC

Published by
**Golden Apple Productions**
8/9 Frith Street, London W1D 3JB, England.

Exclusive Distributors:
**Music Sales Limited**
Distribution Centre, Newmarket Road, Bury St Edmunds, Suffolk IP33 3YB, England.
**Music Sales Corporation**
257 Park Avenue South, New York, NY10010, United States of America.
**Music Sales Pty Limited**
120 Rothschild Avenue, Rosebery, NSW 2018, Australia.

Order No. GA11550
ISBN 1-84449-457-8
This book © Copyright 2004 by Golden Apple Productions.

Cover design by Butterworth Design
Music processed by Camden Music
Printed in the United Kingdom

# Cast

| | |
|---|---|
| **Narrators** | allocate as appropriate |
| **Emperor** | |
| **Chancellor** | (speaking) |
| **3 Tricksters (Rogue Weavers)** | (speaking) |
| **Royal Trumpeters** | |
| **Courtiers** | |
| **Crowds with small flags** | |
| **Child** | (shouting) |

# Props

- Royal throne (chair covered in red cloth)
- Empty box or suitcase
- 3 bags of gold (one for each Trickster)
- Cardboard trumpets
- Three plastic coat hangers
- A cloak to cover the Emperor

# Costumes

No elaborate costumes are required, as appropriate head gear will suffice to denote the characters. For example:

- An imperial crown for the Emperor
- A plumed large flat beret for the Chancellor
- Long chiffon scarves for the female courtiers, draped over pointed paper cones secured with thin elastic around the ears
- Fancy, plush flat beret-type hats for male courtiers
- Red pill-box hats with a side plume for the trumpeters
- Woollen headscarves and rustic caps for the crowds

You may prefer full costuming for a concert presentation.

*All the cast stand to deliver the opening number...*

## Song　People Who Lied

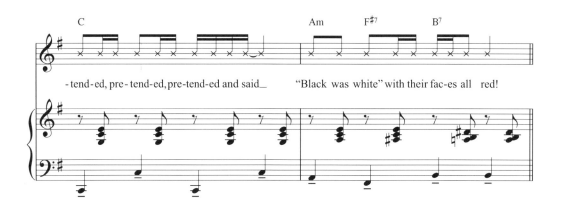

-tend-ed, pre-tend-ed, pre-tend-ed and said__ "Black was white" with their fac-es all red!

This is a stor-y of peo-ple who lied,__ and hid be-hind their sil-ly pride.__ They

*cresc.*

did-n't want to be called a goof,__ so would-n't dare to tell the truth.

*ff*

*The Emperor sits on his throne miming his enjoyment of his morning milkshake treat.*
*The Courtiers are busy talking amongst themselves.*

**NARRATOR:**     The Emperor was having his morning banana milkshake, when three very clever tricksters knocked on the door *(three loud knocks)* and asked to have a word with him.

*The Chancellor goes to the 'door' and returns to the Emperor.*

**CHANCELLOR:**     Your Majesty – three fellows say they have something very, very special just for you.

**NARRATOR:**     So the Emperor agreed to see the three tricksters.

*Emperor nods assent.*
*Enter three Tricksters, dragging an empty box or suitcase.*
*Emperor indicates that the Chancellor and all the Courtiers must leave, and they do.*

**NARRATOR:**     After the Chancellor and the Courtiers had gone, the Emperor leant forward on his throne and asked "Well, what have you got for me?"
The three fellows answered...

**TRICKSTERS:**     Some magic cloth, Your Majesty.

## Song          Tricksters' Song

*During the song the Tricksters open up their box/case and hold up imaginary cloth.*
*They show it off and pretend to feel it. The Emperor is goggle-eyed and has a very funny*
*grimace, as he can't see anything, but pretends that he can. He doesn't want to be a fool!*

**Full of roguish fun** ♩. = 75

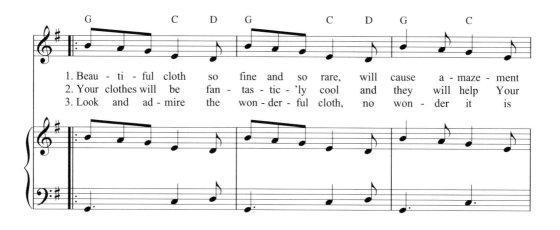

1. Beau - ti - ful cloth so fine and so rare, will cause a - maze - ment
2. Your clothes will be fan - tas - tic - 'ly cool and they will help Your
3. Look and ad - mire the won - der - ful cloth, no won - der it is

ev - 'ry - where. We'll make you clothes with skill and with flare, they'll
Maj - es - ty rule. 'Cause you will sort the wise from the mules, as
cost - ing a lot. Just take a feel, it's soft to the touch and

REFRAIN

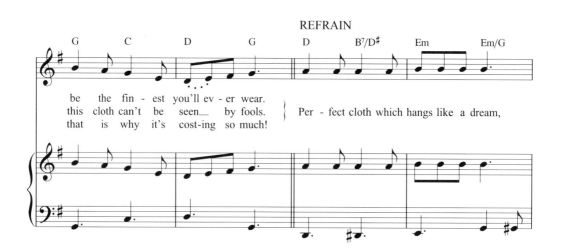

be the fin - est you'll ev - er wear.
this cloth can't be seen__ by fools.    Per - fect cloth which hangs like a dream,
that is why it's cost - ing so much!

**NARRATOR:**

"Well, just how much does the magic cloth cost?" asked the Emperor.

"A suit of royal clothes will cost three bags of gold – all in advance!", replied the Tricksters.

The Emperor said that this was not a problem, and gave the tricksters three bags of gold which he kept under his throne.

"Perhaps this is just a bad day" the Emperor thought, "and when the suit is finished, I'm sure I'll be able to see it".

Repeat

## Song
(See page 3)

# People Who Lied (reprise)

**This is a story of people who lied...**

*All the Court reassembles.*

NARRATOR:     The great day came for the tricksters to deliver the Emperor's new suit. The whole Royal Court was assembled. The Royal Trumpeters played as the Emperor entered and sat on his throne.

*Royal Trumpeters pretend to play their cardboard instruments.*

## Instrumental Royal Fanfare

**Recorders/ocarinas can play the note C'**

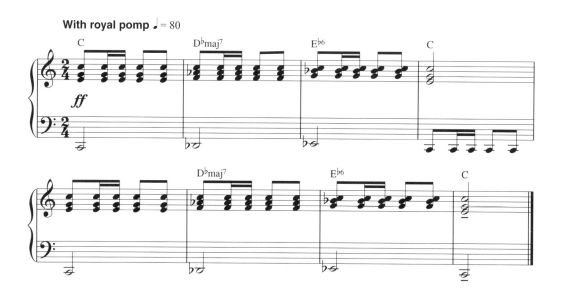

*The three Tricksters enter, dragging their empty box/case.*

**CHANCELLOR:**     Please show us the royal suit.

**NARRATOR:**     The three fellows smiled at the Emperor and asked permission to speak. The Emperor agreed – he was getting very excited about his new clothes. "Remember" said the Tricksters…

**TRICKSTERS:**     This suit can't be seen by fools!

| NARRATOR: | Everyone watched in silence as the three rogues opened up their box and held up three empty coat hangers.<br>They were smiling and admiring a suit of clothes that wasn't there. |
|---|---|
| ONE TRICKSTER: | Is Your Majesty pleased with his suit of clothes? |
| NARRATOR: | The Emperor was too embarrassed and proud to admit that he couldn't actually see the suit. He said "It is magnificent!" as he didn't want to look a fool.<br>The Chancellor agreed, and everyone smiled and said it was the best suit of clothes they had ever seen. No one dared tell the truth. After all, no one wanted to be a fool! |

*The Tricksters exit with the Emperor, taking the box/suitcase and coat hangers with them.*

## Repeat

## Song
(See page 3)

# People Who Lied (reprise)

**This is a story of people who lied...**

| NARRATOR: | A public parade was held that very afternoon. |
|---|---|

*Enter crowds with small flags, making a line. The Courtiers reposition to form part of the crowds.*

| NARRATOR: | How loudly everyone cheered to greet the Emperor as he entered wearing his new suit of clothes. |
|---|---|

*Royal Trumpeters play their cardboard trumpets.*

## Repeat

## Instrumental
(See page 8)

# Royal Fanfare (reprise)

**Recorders/ocarinas can play the note C'**

*The Emperor enters wearing just his underclothes. He proudly processes and acts as though showing off his wonderful new clothes. He looks ridiculous!*

Song  It's Fantastic, Gorgeous!

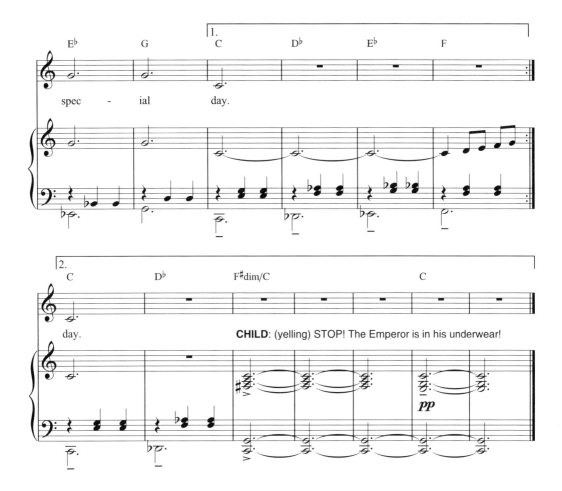

**NARRATOR:** Everything stopped. The crowds looked aghast at the brave little boy. Then they looked at each other, and a loud murmuring went up – everyone including the Emperor realised that they weren't alone in not seeing the suit of clothes. The Emperor's eyes nearly popped out of his head as he realised that he was parading in his underwear!

**CHANCELLOR:** Your Majesty has been taken for a ride. There never was any magic cloth and you've lost your three bags of gold!

**NARRATOR:** The Chancellor called for a cloak to cover the Emperor, and this was put around him. Everyone felt a bit silly and red-faced. But the Emperor puffed up his chest and declared that this had indeed been a very special day, as everyone was wiser and had learnt that it was always best to speak out for what was right. It was obvious that everyone had been made to look like fools.
It wasn't a fool who couldn't see the cloth, it was a fool who said he could!

Song **Tell the Truth**

that aren't true. You're a meg-a fool if that's what you do. Re-

-mem - ber the Emp - 'ror had noth-ing to wear; if it weren't for his un - dies

he'd have been bare! Don't call out "black" when it's real - ly white,

stand up for your-self and    say what's    right.

right.                        (speaking) Tell the truth!

**THE END**

# Recipe for Imperial Mint Sweets

(Remember to check for allergies)

Buy some ready-made white icing. Wash hands thoroughly and work some peppermint essence drops into the icing, by kneading it on a clean bread/chopping board. Using your hands, roll out the icing into sausage shapes and cut up the 'sausages' as if chopping a carrot into rings. Each shape will be one sweet. Pat the sweets into acceptable shapes and leave to dry out, covered with a clean tea towel. Dust generously with icing sugar. To make each sweet exceptionally royal, place a small coloured sweet on the top!

# TWO MAGIC TRICKS
## The Amazing Mind-Reading Feat

- You need to have an accomplice who remains in the room whilst you leave and shut the door. Between yourselves, you had chosen a colour, perhaps green.
- The accomplice chooses someone who picks an item in the room which you will identify when you come back.
- The accomplice opens the door and you return.
- Ask everyone to concentrate on the chosen item, as you will be reading their minds.
- Your accomplice points to things around the room, avoiding pointing to anything green. But when he/she does point to something green, the following object they point to will be the one which you have to identify. This is a simple, yet effective trick.

## The Invisible Secret Message!

- Shave one end of a white household candle into a point, just like a pencil.
- Write or draw a secret message or picture onto a clean piece of white paper.
- Only you will know at this stage what is on the paper, as it will be invisible to others.
- Pass your secret document to your friend.
- Using a water-based coloured paint, your friend should brush over the piece of paper.
- Hey presto! The secret message has been revealed for all to see!

# CD Track Listing

1. **Introduction to *The Emperor's New Clothes* and other Golden Apple Bitesize titles.**

   Includes excerpts from the following:

   ***The Gingerbread Man***
   (Key Stages 1 & Lower 2)
   by Alison Hedger
   Sung by Mike Winsor & Elly Barnes
   *Teacher's Book & CD: GA11539*

   ***The Fisherman's Wife***
   (Key Stages 1 & Lower 2)
   by Alison Hedger
   Sung by Elly Barnes & Mike Winsor
   *Teacher's Book & CD: GA11572*

   ***Bella-Bella Cinderella***
   (Pre-school and Key Stage 1)
   by Alison Hedger
   Sung by Elly Barnes & Mike Winsor
   *Teacher's Book & CD: GA11561*

   ***Complete Story & Songs***

2. **People Who Lied**
3. **Tricksters' Song**
4. **People Who Lied (Reprise)**
5. **Royal Fanfare**
6. **People Who Lied (Reprise)**
7. **Royal Fanfare (Reprise)**
8. **It's Fantastic, Gorgeous!**
9. **Tell The Truth**

   ***Backing Tracks (vocals omitted)***

10. **People Who Lied**
11. **Tricksters' Song**
12. **People Who Lied (Reprise)**
13. **Royal Fanfare**
14. **People Who Lied (Reprise)**
15. **Royal Fanfare (Reprise)**
16. **It's Fantastic, Gorgeous!**
17. **Tell The Truth**

**Narration:** Mike Winsor. **Vocals:** Mike Winsor & Elly Barnes. **Music Arranger:** Rick Cardinali.
CD recorded, mixed and mastered by Jonas Persson & Neil Williams.